The life cycle of a
Bean

Ruth Thomson

PowerKiDS press.

New York

Published in 2008 by The Rosen Publishing Group, Inc.
29 East 21st Street, New York, NY 10010

Copyright © 2008 Wayland/The Rosen Publishing Group, Inc.

First Edition

Photo Credits: All cover images and 1, 4-5, 8, 9, 10, 11, 12, 13, 14, 16, 17, 20, 21, 23 Adam White/naturepl.com; 6 Geoff Dann/ DK Images; 7 Roger Phillips/DK Images; 13 Oxford Scientific Films; 15 Premaphoto/ naturepl.com; 18 John B. Free/naturepl.com; 19Meul/ARCO/naturepl.com; 22 wikipedia/nl:Gebruiker:Rasbak

Library of Congress Cataloging-in-Publication Data

Thomson, Ruth, 1949-
  Bean / Ruth Thomson. -- 1st ed.
     p. cm. -- (Learning about life cycles: The life cycle of a bean)
  Includes index.
  ISBN-13: 978-1-4042-3714-8 (library binding)
  ISBN-10: 1-4042-3714-3 (library binding)
 1. Beans--Juvenile literature. 2. Beans--Development--Juvenile literature. I. Title.
  SB327.T46 2007
  635'.65--dc22

2006033084

Manufactured in China

Contents

Beans grow here

Broad beans are good to eat. People grow them in their gardens or **vegetable plots**. Farmers grow thousands of broad bean plants in enormous fields.

What is a broad bean?

A broad bean is a **seed**. Several grow together inside a pod. The tough, thick skin of the pod protects the beans. The beans we eat are soft and green.

pod

bean

This is what a bean looks like inside.

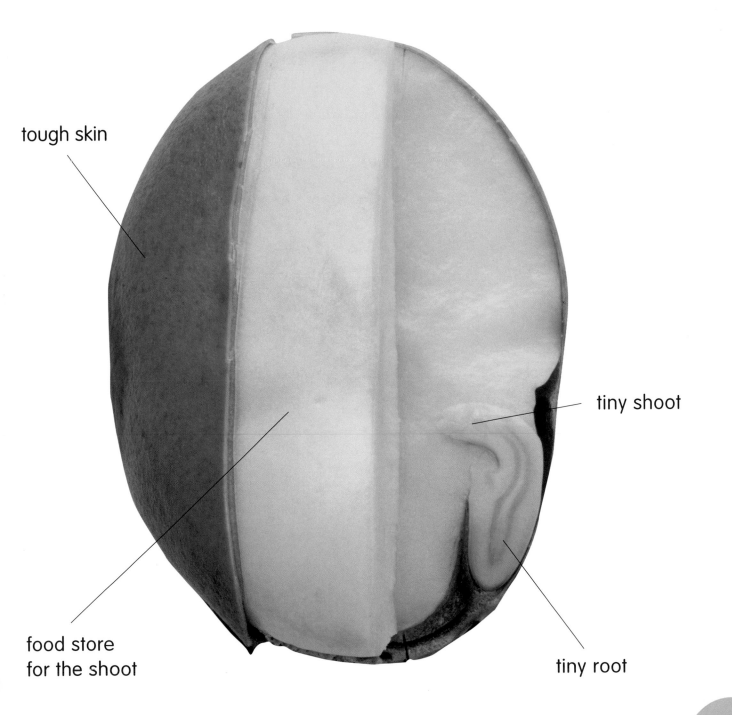

tough skin

tiny shoot

food store
for the shoot

tiny root

Planting

People save a store of beans as seeds for planting. They leave the beans to dry. The beans turn hard and brown.

In the springtime,
the beans are
planted in warm, damp soil.
Water makes the beans swell.

Roots

The hard skin of the bean splits.
A tiny **root** pokes out.
It starts to grow
down into
the soil.

1 week

10

Every day,
the root
grows longer
and longer
and longer.

Shoot

A **shoot** starts to grow upward. On its tip are tiny **leaves**. These bend downward, so they do not break as the shoot pushes through the soil.

2 weeks

The shoot pops out of the soil. The leaves uncurl and turn darker. Side **roots** grow from the main root. Tiny hairs on them take up water from the soil.

3 weeks

6
weeks

Leaves

Now the plant has used up the bean's food store. The **leaves** spread out to catch sunlight. Leaves use water from the soil, sunlight, and air to make food.

Blackfly lay their eggs on the leaves. When the young **hatch,** they eat the leaves. Ladybugs gobble up Black flies, so the leaves do not become too damaged.

10 weeks

Flowers

Every week the plant grows taller and the **leaves** grow bigger. Flower **buds** begin to form.

The buds open out into white flowers. In the center of each flower are tiny grains of yellow **pollen** and a sweet liquid called **nectar**.

12 weeks

Pollination

Bees crawl inside the flowers to sip the **nectar** and collect the **pollen**. The black lines on the petals point the way to the nectar.

As a bee flies from
one flower to another, pollen sticks to
its hairy legs. Pollen from one flower
rubs off onto the next one. This pollen
helps to make new beans.

Beans

Now the flower is no longer needed. Its petals **wither** and fall off, leaving a pod with tiny beans inside.

14 weeks

The beans swell and grow. The pods become long and heavy. People pick the pods before the beans are fully grown, when they are tastiest.

18-20 weeks

24
weeks

New seeds

In the fall, the bean plant shrivels and dies. Unpicked pods turn brown and fall to the ground. Some beans are collected for planting next spring.

Bean life cycle

Bean
The bean is planted.
After 1 week, a
root grows.

Leaves
A **shoot** grows up
out of the soil. The
leaves uncurl.

Bean pods
After 18 weeks, the beans
are ready to be picked.

Flowers
The plant grows taller, and after
12 weeks, flowers appear.

Glossary

bud a swelling on a stem that will grow into a flower or leaves

leaves the part of a plant that makes food

nectar the sweet juice inside a flower

pollen the grains of powder in the center of a flower

root the underground part of a plant that takes in water from the soil

seed the part of a plant that grows into a new plant

shoot the first leaves of a new plant

vegetable plot a small piece of land that people use for growing plants

wither to shrink and dry up

Web Sites
Due to the changing nature of Internet links, PowerKids Press has developed an online list of Web sites related to the subject of this book. This site is regularly updated. Please use this link to access this list: www.powerkidslinks.com/llc/bean/

Index